Red squirrels in my garden

Bernard LELEU

Any resemblance with another squirrel is possible.

Oce upon a time...
a former attractive
house surrounded
by trees,

at the edge of a river, a heavenly place...

Neighbours were very friendly. Some were tall, some small ...

curious,

and these tracks in the fresh snow

They were at their home !

They observed us.

They were

watching us..

We had

to be

accepted...

Squirrels were not the only ihabitants of the garden.

Blue tits, coal tits, great tits, marsh tits, crested tits, long-tailed tits, wrens, nuthatches, treecreepers, robins, finches, blackcaps, etc..

We started with bird nesting boxes,
to protect them from predators...

7

Our little squirrels were not forgotten. We built a large romantic nesting box. It seemed to suit them ...

And another one with a recovery board and a piece of zinc.

9

To gaze at them, I had attached a pot with sunflower seeds. It avoided that they too often go to my neighbour's garden to steal nuts.

On the opposite picture,
you can see the summer hair,
less thick, and denudes ears.

In winter, ears have
long tufts hair with a
nice curling iron effect.

What does it think ?

Are squirrels clever ?
Difficult to assert.
But in the rodent family,
they have a well developed cranial box.

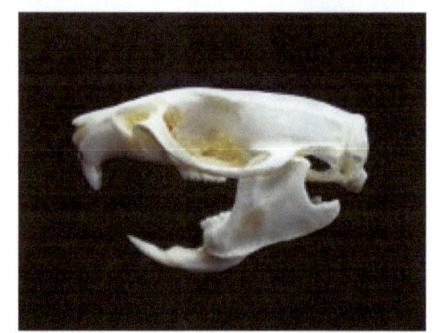

Rat

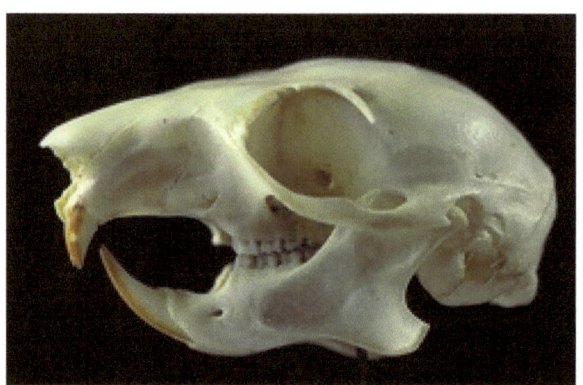

Squirrel

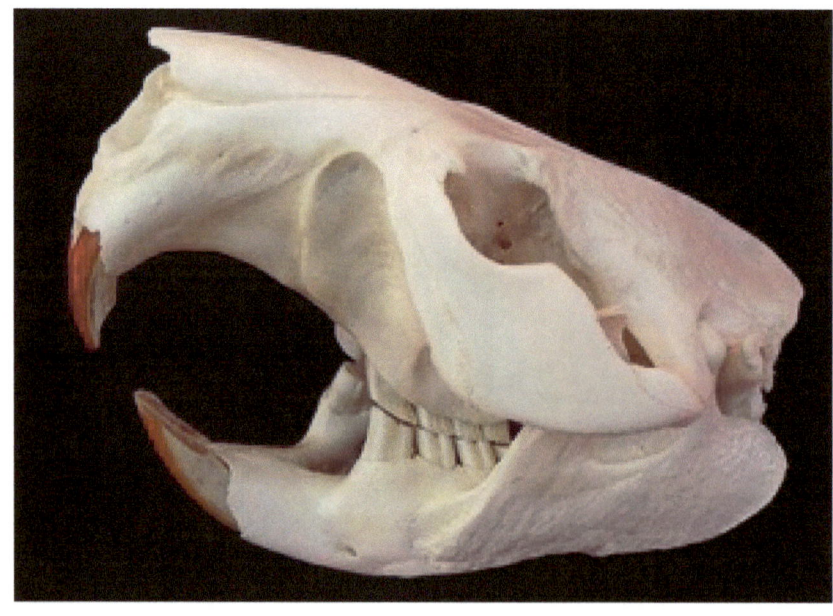

Beaver

View, smelling, hearing ?

They are very sensitive to noises and movements.
They seem to have a selective sense of smell for the reserves they have buried (walnuts, hazelnuts), but they do not perceive the smell of predators. For squirrels, everything still is safe. Moreover, anything behind a window (even in motion) does not frighten them.

Family lunch...

21

What about food ? a little bit of everything...

Hornbean seeds

Walnuts

Hazelnuts

24

Grease balls for birds

Fruits

Vegetables

Sunflower seeds

How to eat ?   four fingers and a small thumb very useful for wedging seeds under the nails !

How to communicate ?

Schieks,

and also with the tail,

which is also a pendulum.

Red, grey-red,
with a black tail,
with white hairs,

They all have white belly.

28

Boys and girls don't have
morphological difference, except ...

29

Last winter, an acacia died, creating a breach in the path. Then a rope was installed to replace the dead tree and allow a passage for squirrels.

Squirrels are players...

... and also curious,

Curiosity punished
by nuthatchs.

Nests

Built in a few days with small branches and moss, high enough to avoid predators (especially martens), not too high to avoid high winds, nests are accessible from the bottom.

Only one day for this one !

Squirrels do not hibernate. They remain hidden in bad weather. They use several nests.

Reproduction.
- Mating in winter (December / January) and spring.
- The males are fertile throughout this period.
- Females are fertile one day during each cycle.
Some datas.
- 1 or 2 litters per year.
- 38 to 40 gestation days.
- 3 to 4 babies, February / April and May / August.
- 2 breastfeeding months.

Babies weigh only 8 to 12 grams at birth. Depending on the outside conditions, they leave the nest after 2 months of breastfeeding. They are adult after 1 year.

In fact, it's difficult to see babies...

To give food to squirrels ?

Yes, to help them in winter. But not too much, even it satisfies our ego. First you have to preserve their habitat !

Some one eat in the dish,

Others are puzzled by the seeds shop...

Roger my neighbour has walnut and hazelnut trees. He harvests 40kg nuts each year.
I tried to reassure Roger by explaining that squirrels don't have a backpack, and that they carried only one by one walnut ...

But every year, we set up a small alternative store, to avoid neighbourhood conflicts.

Opportunist squirrels ?

If you tempte them...

They can't resist !

Always and always...

... facetious.

Always and always...

... exciting.

Today,
Sciurus erectus...

Tomorrow,
Sciurus sapiens ?

A great thank you to all our little neighbours which amuse us each day and which helped me to realize this booklet.

All photos were taken in the garden.

Other photos and videos on the web site http://cotenichoirs.free.fr